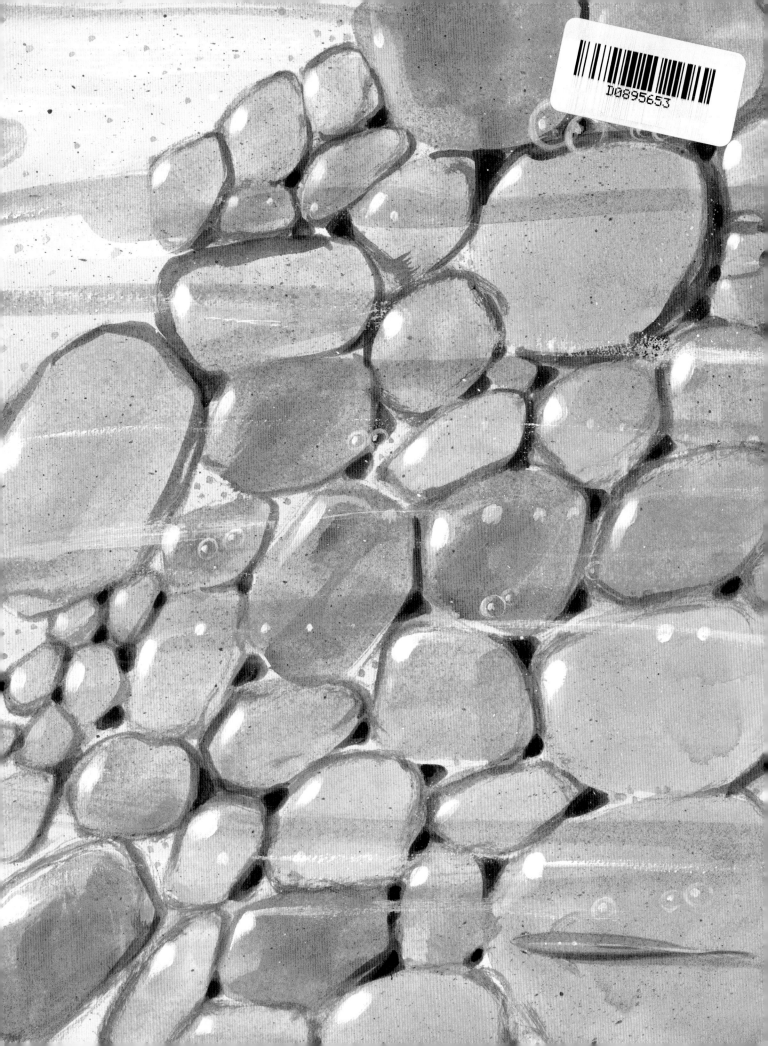

THE BROOK BOOK

exploring the smallest streams

Jim Arnosky

Dutton Children's Books

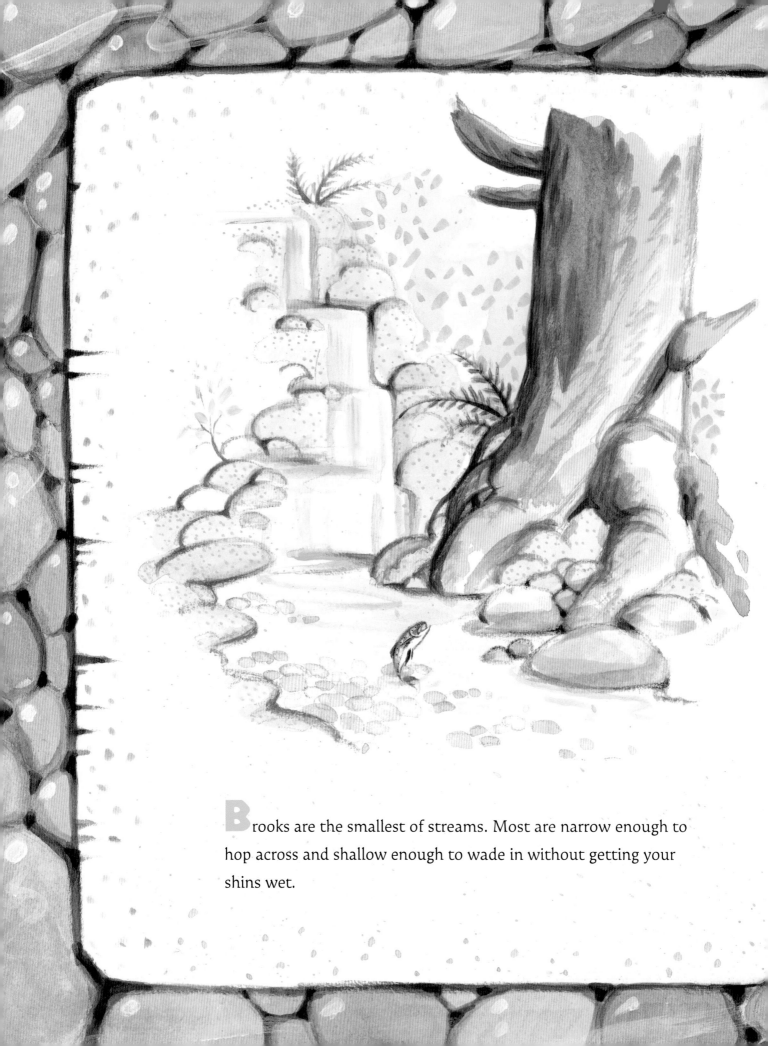

Brooks are the smallest of streams. Most are narrow enough to hop across and shallow enough to wade in without getting your shins wet.

Brook explorers are as curious as raccoons, eager to reach down in the water and feel around to find out what lives there.

Because any water can be deeper than it looks, even the tiniest brooks should be approached carefully. Use a long stick to measure the water's depth and probe the streambed for firmness. If the brook is only a few inches deep and the bottom is firm, you can safely reach in. Feel the texture of the pebbles and sand. Remove small boulders to examine more closely and look for aquatic insects clinging to the wet stones.

WHERE DOES THE WATER IN A BROOK COME FROM?

A brook can begin as a mountain spring flowing out of a hillside or as water seeping up from the ground. Most brooks begin on high ground and flow downhill. Even if it doesn't look slanted, the brook that flows past your home or school is running downhill from its source. The faster the flow, the steeper the brook's course.

Where a brook seeps back into the ground, a beautiful wetland is created.

WHERE DOES THE WATER IN A BROOK GO?

A brook may flow for many miles before seeping back into the ground or joining the flow of a larger stream.

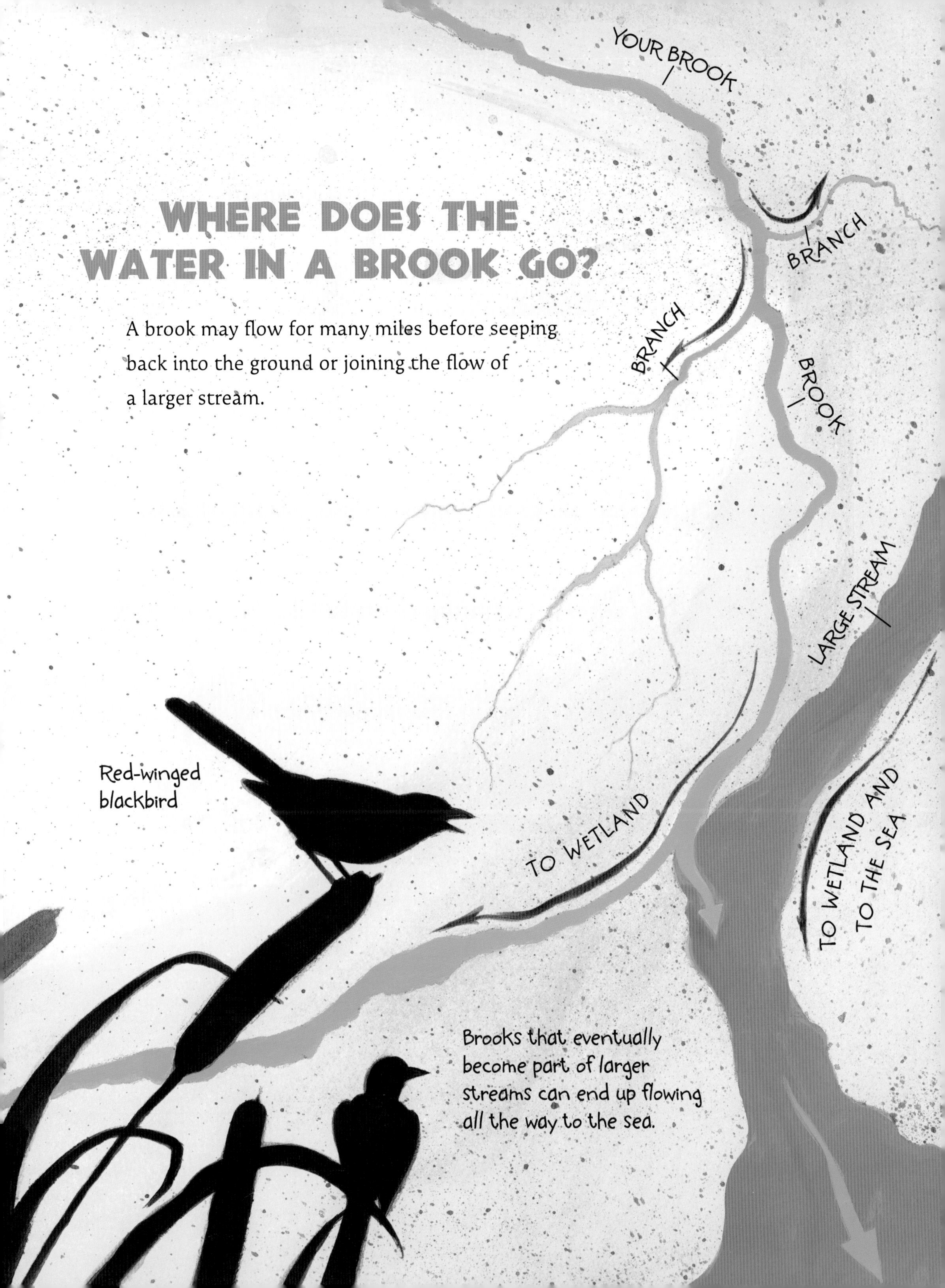

YOUR BROOK

BRANCH

BRANCH

BROOK

LARGE STREAM

TO WETLAND

TO WETLAND AND TO THE SEA

Red-winged blackbird

Brooks that eventually become part of larger streams can end up flowing all the way to the sea.

Even in a tiny brook there is a lot of water flowing by. Heavy rains or melting snow and ice can fill a little brook, making it flow with much more water and force. Never go near a brook during times of high water. Streamside rocks can be slippery, and you can fall into the torrent. A bank undermined by rushing water can collapse when you step on it.

The best time to explore a brook is when the water is low and the stream trickles and ripples gently along. Even then, it's best to stay where the water is only inches deep. Never go exploring on your own. You need a grown-up along for safety.

The complete brook explorer

The complete brook explorer wears rubber boots and carries a fine mesh net for catching flying insects or scooping up water creatures. A clear plastic jar makes a great unbreakable aquarium for temporarily holding your catch.

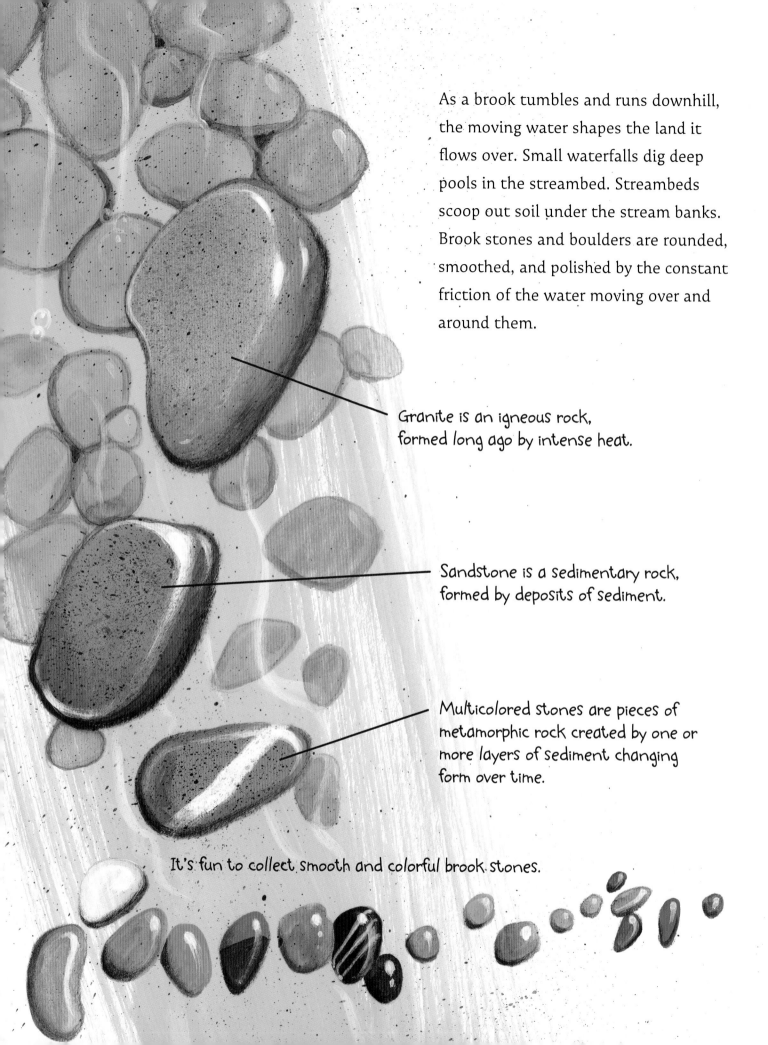

As a brook tumbles and runs downhill, the moving water shapes the land it flows over. Small waterfalls dig deep pools in the streambed. Streambeds scoop out soil under the stream banks. Brook stones and boulders are rounded, smoothed, and polished by the constant friction of the water moving over and around them.

Granite is an igneous rock, formed long ago by intense heat.

Sandstone is a sedimentary rock, formed by deposits of sediment.

Multicolored stones are pieces of metamorphic rock created by one or more layers of sediment changing form over time.

It's fun to collect smooth and colorful brook stones.

Turn over a good-size brook boulder and look closely at the wet surface. Chances are you will see tiny aquatic insects crawling on it. The nymphs, or beginning stages of mayflies, stone flies, and other stream-borne flies, live on submerged rocks, where they feed on microscopic organisms. Nymphs' flat bodies allow them to crawl under and not be crushed by the heavy stream boulders.

You can pick up any nymphs you find. They won't bite. But after holding them in your wet hand for a little while, release them to their boulder and gently place them in the stream in their original positions.

Stone fly adult

Shed nymphal skins

The stone fly begins life in the water, lives as a nymph, and eventually becomes a winged adult. Adult stone flies shed their nymphal skin and emerge completely winged and ready to fly.

stone fly nymph

MAYFLIES

Mayflies are among the most commonly found aquatic insects. The life cycle of a mayfly is the same as that of a stone fly except that, at the time of emergence, most species of mayflies shed their nymphal skin while still in the water.

Mayfly nymph

Adult mayfly

Mayflies come in a variety of sizes, from very small to large. Silhouettes show actual size.

Newly emerged mayflies float on the water until their new wings dry. Then they fly away.

CADDIS FLIES

Caddis flies are aquatic insects that live the first part of their lives underwater as larvae. A caddis fly larva looks like a small white grub. Caddis flies protect their soft bodies by building hard cases in which they live until it is time for them to emerge as winged adults.

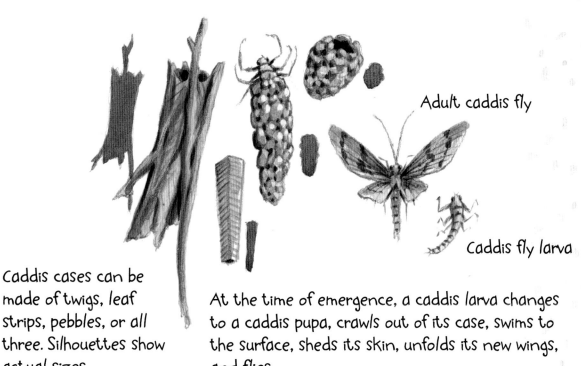

Adult caddis fly

Caddis fly larva

Caddis cases can be made of twigs, leaf strips, pebbles, or all three. Silhouettes show actual sizes.

At the time of emergence, a caddis larva changes to a caddis pupa, crawls out of its case, swims to the surface, sheds its skin, unfolds its new wings, and flies.

SKETCHING WILDFLOWERS

Wildflowers grow in the moist soil of a brook's banks. Don't pick the flowers you see. Leave them for others to enjoy. Sketching wildflowers is one way you can bring the flowers home without picking any.

Dog-toothed trillium

Drawing a wildflower is easy. Begin with the stem.
Add the leaves. Then finish with the flower.

Here are five wildflowers that you might see growing on the banks of a brook.

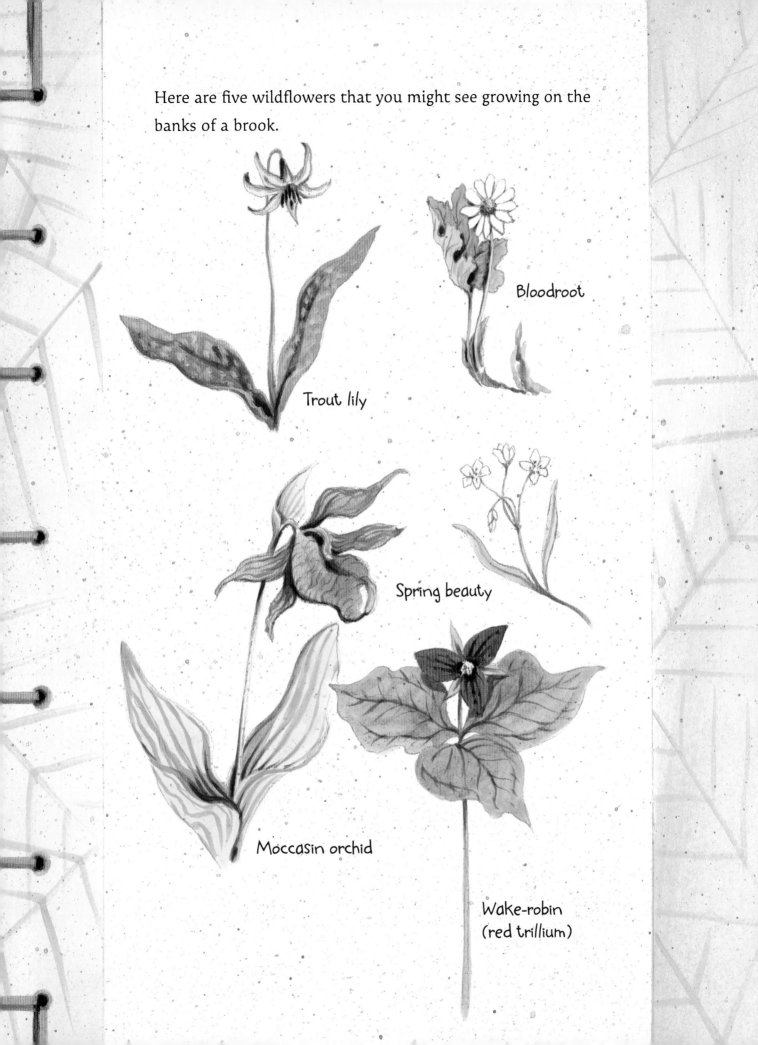

Trout lily

Bloodroot

Spring beauty

Moccasin orchid

Wake-robin
(red trillium)

Tweezers

Fine
mesh net

COLLECTING

Hold a fine mesh net in the brook for a
minute, and you may catch some small
aquatic insects adrift in the current. A
white refrigerator tray with a half inch
or so of water makes a great holding
tank. All the creatures you catch will
be dark and easy to see against the
white pan.

Catch flying insects with your mesh
net, and put your catch in a clear
plastic jar. Don't forget to poke some
airholes in the lid.

Plastic jar

Refrigerator tray

Shed
nymphal skins in
a small spice jar

Crayfish are small freshwater cousins of lobsters. They live in the slowest-moving sections of brooks, where they crawl on the brook's stony bottom.

The hard outer skeleton of a crayfish is made of chitin (pronounced ky-tin). Their chitin armor protects crayfish as they bulldoze under small stones in their hunt for food.

Catch a crayfish with your net. They have strong, sharp claws that can pinch your hand.

Salamanders live under the wet leaves, stones, and debris that collect on brook banks. You can catch small salamanders with your hands. They won't bite. Hold them gently in a wet hand or a wet tray. As with all your catches, keep them only long enough to look at them closely. Then release them where you found them.

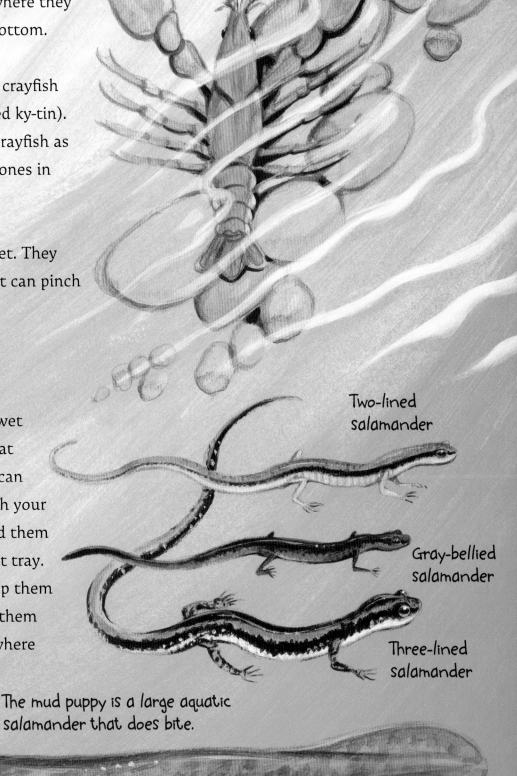

Two-lined salamander

Gray-bellied salamander

Three-lined salamander

The mud puppy is a large aquatic salamander that does bite.

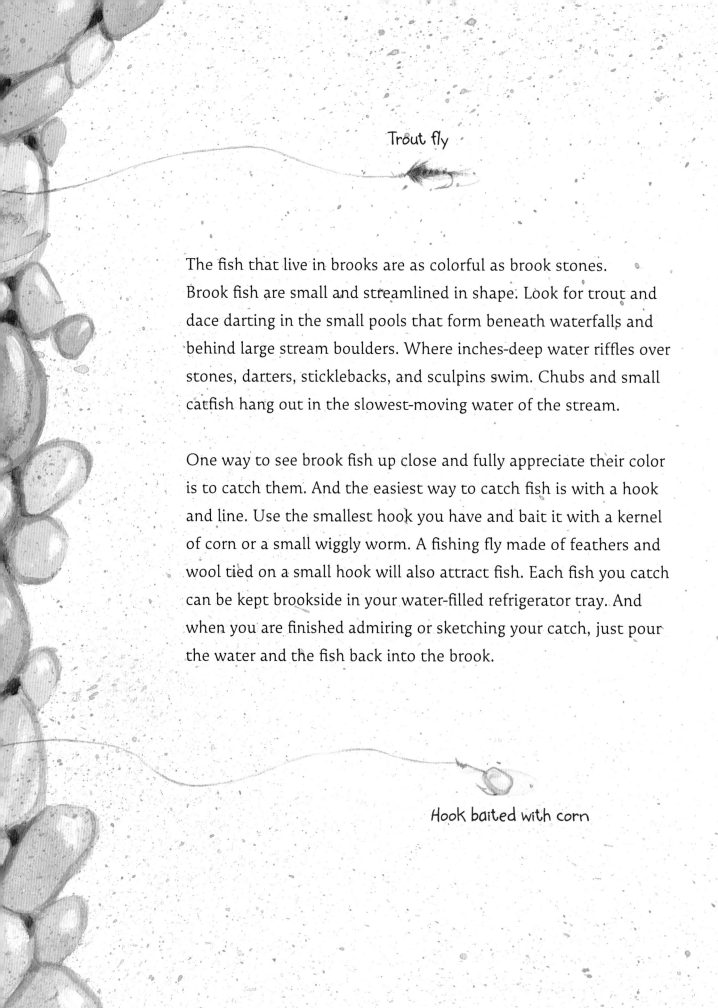

Trout fly

The fish that live in brooks are as colorful as brook stones. Brook fish are small and streamlined in shape. Look for trout and dace darting in the small pools that form beneath waterfalls and behind large stream boulders. Where inches-deep water riffles over stones, darters, sticklebacks, and sculpins swim. Chubs and small catfish hang out in the slowest-moving water of the stream.

One way to see brook fish up close and fully appreciate their color is to catch them. And the easiest way to catch fish is with a hook and line. Use the smallest hook you have and bait it with a kernel of corn or a small wiggly worm. A fishing fly made of feathers and wool tied on a small hook will also attract fish. Each fish you catch can be kept brookside in your water-filled refrigerator tray. And when you are finished admiring or sketching your catch, just pour the water and the fish back into the brook.

Hook baited with corn

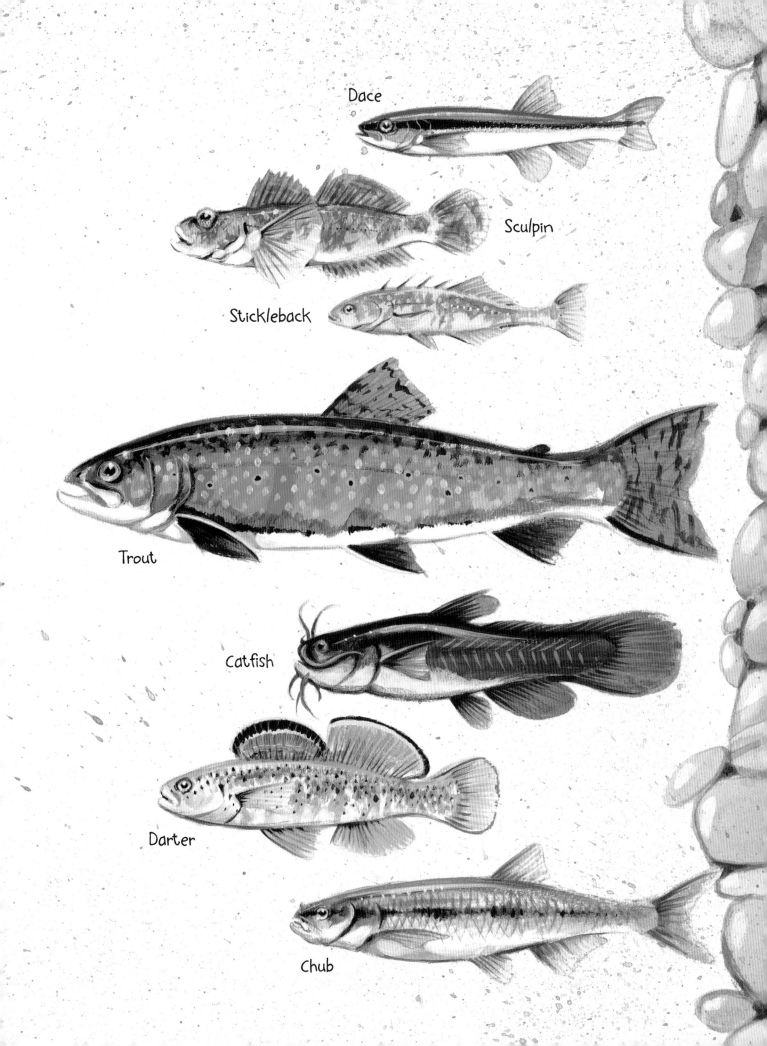

Dace

Sculpin

Stickleback

Trout

Catfish

Darter

Chub

BROOKSIDE BIRDS

While catching fish, netting aquatic insects, and collecting smooth and colorful stones, don't forget to look up. Many beautiful birds inhabit brookside brush and trees.

You won't need binoculars to watch these birds closely. Just sit on the brook bank and birds will come very close to you. Here are some of the birds you may see along your favorite brook.

Yellow-throated warbler

Waterthrush

Wood thrush

In the birds shown, males and females are similar, except for the nuthatch.

Chickadee

White-breasted nuthatch

A female nuthatch
has a gray cap.

The pileated woodpecker is
our largest woodpecker.
The downy woodpecker is
our smallest.

Pileated woodpecker

Downy woodpecker

The pileated woodpeckers are the
only woodpeckers that make large
rectangular holes in trees.

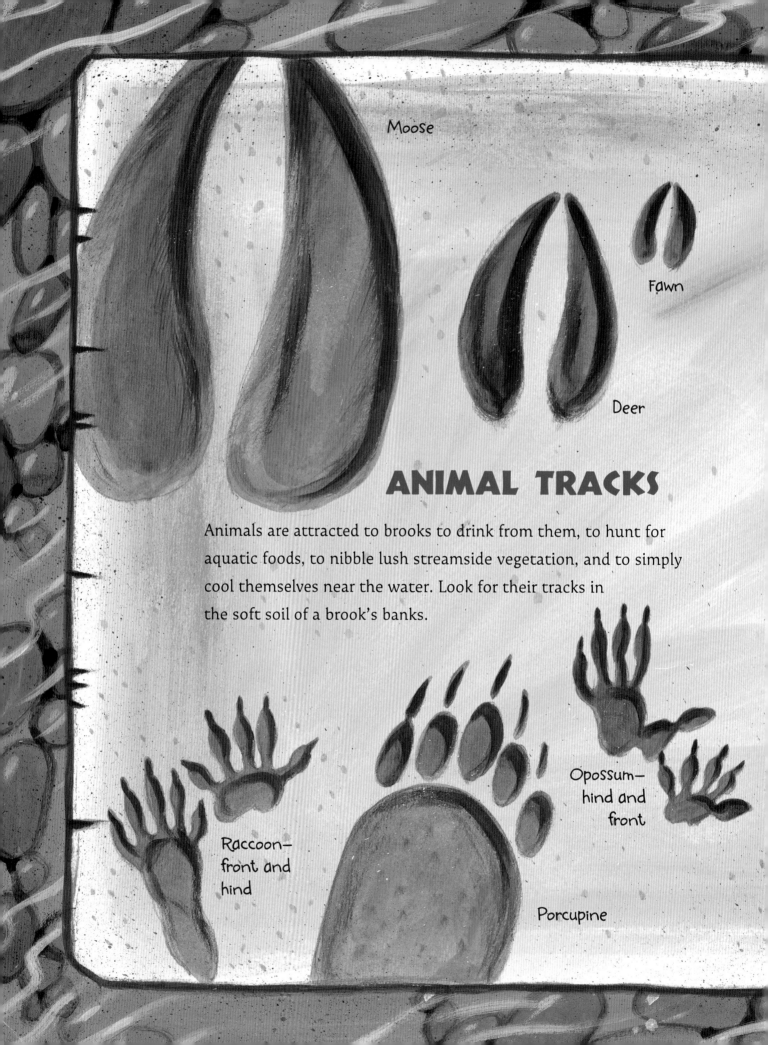

Moose

Fawn

Deer

ANIMAL TRACKS

Animals are attracted to brooks to drink from them, to hunt for aquatic foods, to nibble lush streamside vegetation, and to simply cool themselves near the water. Look for their tracks in the soft soil of a brook's banks.

Opossum—
hind and
front

Raccoon—
front and
hind

Porcupine

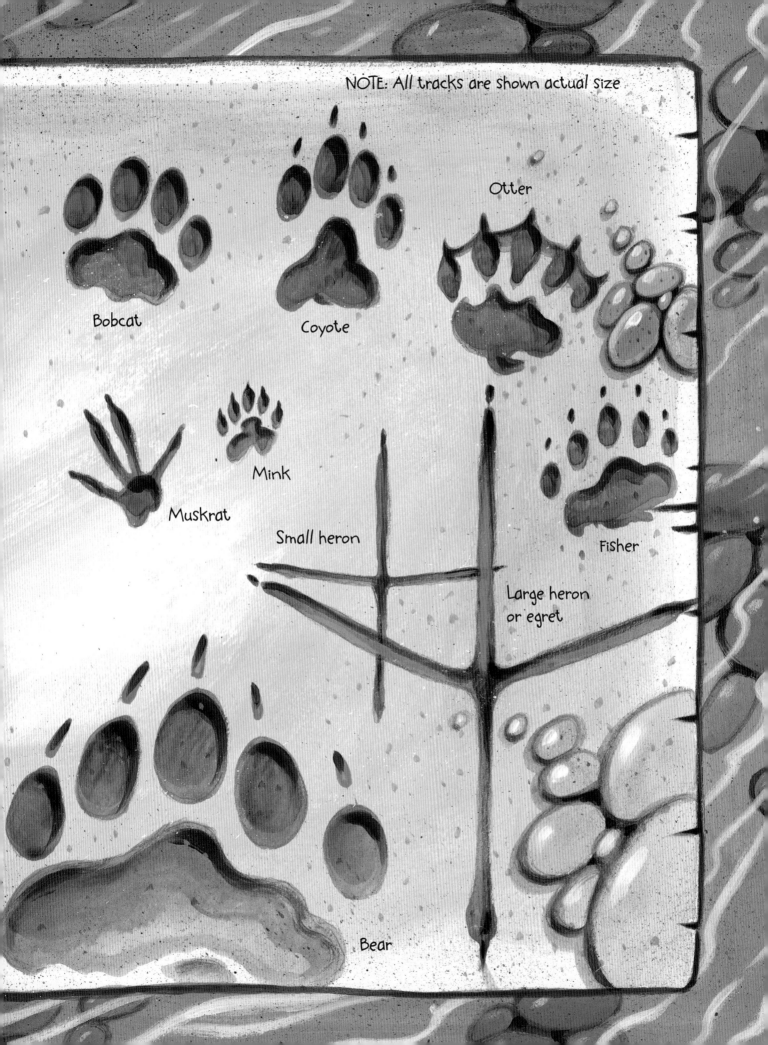

If you're lucky, you will see a maker of tracks quietly walking beside the brook or peacefully drinking in the stream.

A brook is an inviting place. It calls you with its babbling sound. It sparkles and glows. It cools you as it flows by. And it quenches your thirst for nature in its wildest form.

AUTHOR'S NOTE

The Brook Book is organized in such a way as to help you get the most out of your class visit to a favorite brook. By visiting a brook, children can learn about water, rocks, aquatic insects, fish, amphibians, environmental issues, and more. Using The Brook Book can help you to identify many of the things you and your students might see in a brook. It illustrates the simple tools and safe techniques for catching and collecting small aquatic animals, and it encourages the gentle release of the animals to their original location in or near the stream. Teachers can bring the lessons they learn afield back to the classroom by using a detailed topographical map and a yellow Magic Marker to trace their neighborhood brook to its source and determine where it ultimately flows.

I urge all parents and teachers to include visits to these smallest of streams on their weekend hikes and afternoon outdoor educational classes. Discover what makes your local brook unique. It could be the types of stones, the lack of stones, the clarity of water, the number of small falls or pools, or its species of resident fish. I encourage teachers to emphasize safety as well as exploration. Learn and teach your students how to distinguish when the local brook is safe to explore and when it is running too high and fast to approach.

Finally, have your class research the origin of your brook's name. It's a great way to learn more about its natural history and perhaps even a little about the history of your region.

Jim Arnosky

MORE BOOKS FOR BROOK EXPLORERS AND NATURALISTS

Arnosky, Jim. *All About Frogs*. New York: Scholastic, 2002.

—. *All About Lizards*. New York: Scholastic, 2004.

—. *All About Turtles*. New York: Scholastic, 2000.

Baker, Nick. *Rivers, Ponds, and Lakes*. New York: Harpercollins, 2007.

Beatty, Richard. *Rivers, Lakes, Streams, and Ponds*. Chicago: Heinemann-Raintree, 2003.

Donovan, Sandra. *Animals of Rivers, Lakes, and Ponds*. Chicago: Heinemann-Raintree, 2003.

Lindeen, Carol. *Life in a Stream*. Mankato, MN: Capstone Press, 2003.

Morrison, Gordon. *A Drop of Water*. New York: Houghton Mifflin, 2006.

Parker, Steve. *Eyewitness: Pond & River*. New York: DK Publishing, 2005.

Pascoe, Elaine. *The Ecosystem of a Stream*. New York: Rosen Publishing Group, 2003.

Royston, Angela. *My World of Geography: Rivers*. Chicago: Heinemann Library, 2005.

Taylor, Barbara. *Pond and River Life*. Hauppauge, NY: Barron's Educational Series, 2000.

Wechsler, Doug. *Frog Heaven: Ecology of a Vernal Pool*. Honesdale, PA: Boyds Mills Press, 2006.

For Cecily, Michaela, Mason, and Mitchell

DUTTON CHILDREN'S BOOKS
A division of Penguin Young Readers Group

Published by the Penguin Group
Penguin Group (USA) Inc., 375 Hudson Street, New York, New York 10014, U.S.A.
Penguin Group (Canada), 90 Eglinton Avenue East, Suite 700, Toronto, Ontario, Canada M4P 2Y3
(a division of Pearson Penguin Canada Inc.) • Penguin Books Ltd, 80 Strand, London WC2R 0RL, England
Penguin Ireland, 25 St Stephen's Green, Dublin 2, Ireland (a division of Penguin Books Ltd) • Penguin Group
(Australia), 250 Camberwell Road, Camberwell, Victoria 3124, Australia (a division of Pearson Australia
Group Pty Ltd) • Penguin Books India Pvt Ltd, 11 Community Centre, Panchsheel Park, New Delhi - 110 017,
India • Penguin Group (NZ), 67 Apollo Drive, Rosedale, North Shore 0632, New Zealand (a division of Pearson
New Zealand Ltd) • Penguin Books (South Africa) (Pty) Ltd, 24 Sturdee Avenue, Rosebank, Johannesburg 2196,
South Africa Penguin Books Ltd, Registered Offices: 80 Strand, London WC2R 0RL, England

CIP Data is available.

Published in the United States by Dutton Children's Books,
a division of Penguin Young Readers Group
345 Hudson Street, New York, New York 10014
www.penguin.com/youngreaders

Designed by Abby Kuperstock

Manufactured in China • First Edition
ISBN 978-0-525-47716-7
1 3 5 7 9 10 8 6 4 2